CANDLES

A Modern Guide to Making Candles

Ebi & Emmanuel Sinteh

Contents

Introduction

EVER SINCE WE CAN REMEMBER, both as individuals and as a couple, we have loved the feeling of coming home, returning to an environment that makes you *feel* happy, at peace, or just makes you feel *something*. There is no better feeling than arriving home after a long day, lighting a candle and relaxing. Or, if you're a morning person, waking up, putting together breakfast and settling down to enjoy it by candlelight. These little details and moments make a home come to life.

In setting up our own home, we quickly realized the huge part that candles and scent play in creating an ambience within your space. In fact, looking back, so many memories for us are locked in scent. From Emmanuel's late nights studying at university in Nigeria by candlelight during power cuts, to when we moved into our first flat together in Aberdeen and went shopping for essentials (aka scented candles!). Over the past few years, we have all spent a lot of time within our homes and really begun to understand the joy that can be found within those four walls, when you intentionally make celebrating your space a priority and create a home with details that bring you joy.

The concept of celebrating the home became the catalyst and ethos for Our Lovely Goods, with candles being the cornerstone of what we do.

We had always dreamed of starting a business together and during Ebi's maternity leave it felt like the perfect time to try our hands at something and really give it a go. We constantly had candles burning in the house but hadn't ever looked into making them. After lots of research our kitchen soon became a production site and testing began. We weren't sure what our brand would become but one thing we were clear on was the fact that we wanted to create candles with scents inspired by a story, transporting people to a moment or place.

After much trial and error, experimentation with wax, wicks, oils, troubleshooting 'scented candles' with no scent, we finally got the hang of it. And so, Our Lovely Goods was born. Our brand is really an extension of us and weaves together our passions for home, family and heritage.

Our initial range consisted of four candle scents, all inspired by a special place or pivotal moment in our life. It was an amazing and surprisingly emotional experience coming up with scents that we felt reflected special memories. First in our range was a candle we called The Month of May. May 2018 held a lot of significance for us; it was the month our first daughter was born and also the month that Ebi's father unexpectedly passed away, just a few days after she gave birth. Through the pain that we felt during that time, the birth of our first daughter was a light that kept us going. And so, in creating this candle we chose to use oils with fresh and mood-boosting scents, like May Chang and Basil. We know Ebi's dad would have wanted us to find some joy through the pain of losing him, so we felt a bright and invigorating scent was perfect to reflect this. Another of our first scents was the Road to Port Harcourt candle, inspired by Emmanuel's home town, Port Harcourt, Nigeria. The scent is deep and earthy with grassy notes of Vetiver and spice from Black Pepper, reflecting the city where Emmanuel spent so many early years of his life.

This is what makes candle making so special to us. The ability to create feelings or bring back memories through scent is a magical thing.

We launched online in 2019 and since then we have seen our candles and wider range stocked all over the world – from Scotland where we live and further afield across the UK, to Finland and Austria, and even as far as Taiwan. It's such a thrill to see products we are so passionate about in so many homes worldwide. We have also had the honour of teaching hundreds of people the art and science of candle making through workshops and events.

Finding joy in expressing ourselves through scent and sharing this through our brand is really a dream and, in this book, we wanted to share that joy with you and encourage you to celebrate the feeling of home through candles and fragrance. It's such a simple way to enhance everyday moments, and the pride you feel when you have created a beautiful candle with your own hands is immense. Additionally, we want you to think of candles as a key aspect of your home interiors.

How to Use This Book

This book will guide you through the fundamentals of making candles. From scented jar candles, to tealights and taper candles. We will walk you through everything we have learnt about wax, essential oils, fragrance oils, wicks and blending. We've included fun projects for you to begin your candle-making discovery, and focused on how you can live in tune with the seasons through the scents and ingredients you use.

In the second chapter, Candle Making 101, you will learn the building blocks of candle making, giving you the confidence to try your hand at the projects that follow. The techniques used in candle making are relatively simple, however the art and science of candle making cannot be mastered simply by reading about the techniques. To perfect your craft, a process of trial and error and good note taking is required.

The remainder of the book has been broken down into seasons. At the start of each chapter, we have suggested some of our favourite fragrances to use for candle making at that time of year, and our preferred types of candles to use for that season: think taper candles for summer evenings and dinner with friends (see page 76); crackling wooden wick candles for autumnal afternoons (see page 110); or fragrant aromatherapy candles, celebrating spring botanicals.

People often think of candles as purely a special treat for autumn and winter but we believe that candles can and should be enjoyed year-round.

Scent & Memory

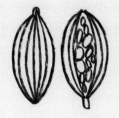

The Science of Smell

Now, we are by no means neuroscientists (although Ebi did study pharmacy in another life) but it has long been documented that scent can serve as a memory trigger, enhancing our ability to recall or recognize information. This is due to the olfactory system of the brain which is involved in regulating emotion and _emotional memories_. Olfactory memories (memories triggered by smell) are often described as involuntary memory – the link between the trigger scent and the memory can sometimes be deep, complex and hard to describe.

Olfactory memories differ from other types of memory due to the strong link to emotional memories. The olfactory nerve is right beside the amygdala (a part of the brain responsible for particular emotions) and a few synapses away from the hippocampus (which is responsible for long-term memory). Studies have shown that olfactory memory is also very resistant to forgetting, as the memories remain deeply ingrained within.

The Proustian Moment

In the twentieth century, Marcel Proust, a writer, eloquently described the phenomenon of a memory triggered by a sensory experience. In his work, _À La Recherche du Temps Perdu (Remembrance of Things Past)_, Proust says the following:

'... I carried to my lips a spoonful of the tea in which I had let soften a bit of madeleine. But at the very instant when the mouthful of tea mixed with cake crumbs touched my palate, I quivered, attentive to the extraordinary thing that was happening inside me. I had ceased to feel I was mediocre, contingent, mortal. Where could it have come to me from – this powerful joy? I sensed that it was connected to the taste of the tea and the cake, but that it went infinitely far beyond it, could not be of the same nature. Where did it come from? What did it mean? How could I grasp it?'

In this passage, Proust describes how the taste of the madeleine brought back fond memories of a time in his childhood, spending the summer in his aunt's house, where she used to serve him madeleines dipped in tea. This literary description soon became known as The Proustian Moment – _'the sudden, involuntary evocation of an emotional memory'._

Both with our business ethos and when developing scent blends and names, we focus on how the aromas make us feel, what they remind us of, or what emotion or memory we are trying to evoke. At the beginning of our journey it was all quite intuitive and we weren't really aware of the science behind it all, but it has been fascinating to learn about the ways science, scent and emotion are all interlinked.

Emmanuel

*The common thread running through everything we
do is our Nigerian heritage. We both come from a culture
rooted in gathering family, sharing food, good music
and a laid-back approach to life. Nigeria is a big source
of inspiration for us, the sensory overload of colours,
textures and the unforgettable people.*

Growing up in Port Harcourt, Nigeria, shaped me in so many ways – it's a rugged town, with a lot of buzz. PH, as we fondly call it, isn't for the faint-hearted. But, if you were born and raised there, you will be familiar with the soft side of it that isn't necessarily apparent on the surface.

Food is a constant theme in memories of my upbringing, and the aromatics and spices linked to meals I loved. Growing up, I spent a lot of time with my mum and sisters in the kitchen, and was always amazed at the way they layered flavours into our meals using herbs, spices and roots. I marvelled at their craft and how the aroma suddenly enveloped the house and elevated my soul even at a young age. Unbeknownst to me, this created my love for scent and how it can affect your mood and feed your soul.

Another strong memory for me was the rainy season – I wondered at how the precipitation hit the ground, releasing that warm, earthy smell into the air and how the trees and bushes blossomed, drawing the butterflies and birds towards them. As a young boy, in between games, I would pluck a small bunch of fresh greenery or flowers and leave them in my shorts' pocket so that every time I dipped my hand in and out, I could catch a whiff of their fresh herbaceous aroma.

Fast forward twenty-something years, and I found myself building a life in the north east of Scotland, yet these memories of scent still stay with me and guide my approach to fragrance, candle making and filling our home with memory and beautiful scent.

Epi

Home should be a place where you can be completely at ease. Somewhere to shut the door on the stresses and pressures of the outside world, where it's OK to wear pyjamas all day, eat cereal at the kitchen counter and call it dinner, and dance to your favourite track, loudly, on repeat.

From a young age, scent has been inextricably linked with my memory. I vividly remember the scent of our first home in Scotland, a few thousand miles away from Nigeria where I was born. Scuffling behind my parents, I climbed up the steps and gazed at the granite house, the grey stone catching the light and glimmering. My father unlocked the door, seemingly to a new world. After the initial shock from how chilly the house was, the faint but distinctive scent of the natural wood floors hovered in the air as my brothers and I scurried from room to room.

There was a study downstairs that grew to be my favourite place to play and daydream. I strongly associate that room with the scent of crayons and paper – I often have flashbacks of gazing out of the study window onto the garden. During the spring and summer months, the window would often be open and in would waft the aroma of our garden – the scent of cut grass, budding bushes and hedges, new flowers – and the sense of anticipation for sunny days ahead.

As an introvert, home has always been my sanctuary. Early on in my life I realized how you can create a space that makes you feel cocooned and safe through many mediums such as fabrics, furnishings and, of course, scent. I often had candles and tealights lit in my bedroom as I adored that feeling of walking into a room that smells amazing. As a young girl I never once thought that I would grow up and make candles for a living but it's funny how life's winding journeys lead you to futures you never considered.

Our business has always hinged on the way that scent can make you feel, on how little things make a home, and on celebrating moments and memories that bring you joy. In this book we hope you enjoy embarking on projects that are not only fun to do but also teach you to create candles and scents that you love – and to reminisce on fond scent memories from throughout your life.

SCENT & MEMORY

Candle Making 101

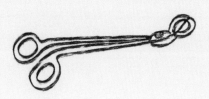

Wax

When making candles, one of the most important considerations is the type of wax you use: the form it comes in and the base ingredients. Your choice of wax will depend on several factors, including the type of candles you would like to make, the kind of wax you would prefer to use (for example, is using an all-natural wax important to you?), the amount of scent throw* you'd like the candle to have, the level of difficulty that you want the project to offer, and even the type of finish you would like to see on your candles. Taking the time to consider all of these factors will help you decide which wax is right for your project.

What is a Candle?

At its core, a candle is a block of fuel (the wax) wrapped around a wick that is ignited, burning the fuel to produce light, warmth and, sometimes, scent. In times gone by, candles were primarily a functional item, used as a source of light. More recently, candles have become a key element of home decor and this has encouraged the development of new techniques and materials.

*The scent throw is the strength of fragrance that the candle releases into the air. Cold throw is the strength of scent when the candle is not lit yet. Hot throw is the strength of the scent throw when the candle is lit and burning.

Wax Forms

BLOCKS

Available as blocks of wax in a rectangular form. This format can be difficult to measure, as any measurement less than the block weight means you need to break the slab into smaller, more manageable chunks. Additionally, because of the reduced surface area of the blocks, they generally take longer to melt than other forms, but do require less storage space.

FLAKES

These are small, irregular flakes of wax. The flat, wide flakes have a high surface area, which means that they melt fast and easily, and are also simple to measure out and weigh the quantity you need.

PELLETS

Wax pellets or beads are similar to flakes in the way they are used and packaged but are shaped in a bead formation. One benefit of this is that they are very resistant to condensation, which can affect your candle-making process or finished candle.

BEESWAX SHEETS

These are beeswax honeycomb sheets that are originally used as foundation sheets for honeycomb, however these can be used for candle making by rolling the sheet around a length of raw wick.

Wax Types

SOY WAX

Soy wax is one of the more recent waxes on the candle-making scene. It was developed in the early 1990s from hydrogenated soybean oil as a response to the growing demand for natural candles. This is our wax of choice due to its ease of use with most fragrances, and high performance in container candles. Additionally, this wax is clean burning, meaning it doesn't emit harmful toxins, and burns slower than other waxes, meaning your candle lasts for longer, too!

BEESWAX

Beeswax is probably the oldest candle-making wax, used by ancient civilizations across the world. This wax is great for making candles that won't be housed in a container, such as pillar or tapered candles, as it is one of the stronger waxes when set.

PARAFFIN WAX

Paraffin wax, or 'mineral' wax, is derived from refined petroleum. It is a fairly inexpensive wax and is used widely in commercial candle making because it can hold a high amount of fragrance and colour. It comes in various melt points, making it suitable for making different types of candles, from containers to pillars.

RAPESEED WAX

Derived from the rapeseed plant, this is a natural vegetable wax. It has similar properties to soy wax, however it has a lower melting point, which means it is a softer wax than soy or paraffin.

COCONUT WAX

Coconut wax is one of the newer waxes on the candle-making scene. It is soft, creamy and white, and, similar to rapeseed wax, it has a low melting point and also often performs well when blending with another wax.

PALM WAX

Derived from the carnauba palm, palm wax is produced by hydrogenating palm oils and is yellow in colour and available as flakes. It is favoured in candle making particularly for pillar and tealight candles, and holds colour and fragrance well.

Wax Blends

Blended candle waxes are made by combining waxes to get the most out of the positive properties found in each wax. Paraffin is often blended with natural waxes such as soy, rapeseed and coconut. Additionally, you can also find natural wax blends that are combinations of 100 per cent naturally derived waxes.

Melting Wax – Double-boiler Method

We use the double-boiler method for melting wax. Remember to only use your equipment (see page 45) for candle making and not repurpose it for food preparation afterward.

Place the metal pouring jug or a heatproof bowl on your scale and tare the weight. Weigh out the specified amount of wax into the jug and place the jug into a saucepan half-filled with water and heat until simmering. Stir with a wooden spoon or spatula until the wax has melted. Once the wax is completely melted, remove the jug or bowl from the heat and rest it on a heatproof surface. You can now add your fragrance and/or dye following the instructions in the project.

Candle Types
and Wax Pairings

Pillar Candles

These candles stand on their own, without the need for a container or candlestick.

The best waxes to create pillar candles are paraffin, beeswax and palm wax. You can also use wax blends to make pillar candles.

Container Candles

These candles are created inside a container, such as a glass jar, a metal tin or a ceramic dish. Because they are very stable, you can use a variety of waxes to make them.

Suitable waxes for container candles include soy wax, soy/paraffin blends, paraffin, palm wax and beeswax.

Moulded Candles

These candles are made in silicon moulds and can be any shape and size.

Best waxes for moulded candles are soy wax, rapeseed wax, coconut wax and wax blends.

Taper Candles

These candles are long and narrow, tapering toward the top with a wider, cylindrical base. They require candlesticks to hold and display them and are elegant options for entertaining or adding classic style to your decor.

The best waxes for making tapered candles are paraffin and beeswax.

Tealight Candles

Tealights are small candles, about 4cm (1½in.) in diameter and about 2cm (¾in.) high, that are designed to sit inside a small, cylindrical metal or clear plastic container.

You can make tealights using most waxes, including soy, palm, paraffin and beeswax, and soy/paraffin blends.

Wicks

Wicks are one of the most important parts of crafting a well-made candle. Essentially, a wick is a porous bundle of fibres that is ignited when lit, carrying fuel to the flame. The most common wick material is cotton (our wick of choice) but wooden wicks are also becoming increasingly popular as they give off a delightful crackling sound when burnt.

We could potentially write a whole book just on wicks as there are thousands of wick types, brands and wick mechanisms out there. Our best advice is to follow the wick guides from the supplier websites when purchasing your wicks. We suggest buying a few wicks at a time to test when creating your candle – the only way to really know if you have the right wick is through lots and lots of testing!

Choosing the Right Wick

When choosing a wick for your candle, there are a few fundamentals that you need to consider:

DIAMETER OF THE CANDLE OR CANDLE CONTAINER

This is one of the most important aspects of choosing the right wick. Use a ruler to measure the diameter of the vessel you wish to use. Typically, the larger the diameter the larger the wick size, or the more wicks you will need.

TYPE OF WAX

Each candle wax type has a different melting point and density, therefore a different wick type will be needed depending on the variances.

FRAGRANCE LOAD AND DYE

It is also important to consider the amount of fragrance or colour (dye) you plan to add to the candle (see page 42). The more colour or fragrance, the thicker the wick needs to be.

Different wick sizes allow for different amounts of wax to be drawn into the flame. If there is too much wax the flame will flare and soot. However, if there is too little fuel then the flame will be extinguished on its own.

When you have chosen the right wick, you will notice it has the following qualities:

- A consistent flame – no self-extinguishing
- An even melt pool across the diameter of the candle
- Maintains a safe, moderate temperature
- No sooting while burning
- A small, safe flame (not too high, minimal flickering)
- A clean burn (doesn't stick to the sides of the jar, if a container candle)

Wick Types

PRE-TABBED

These wicks are cut to different sizes with a metal tab at the bottom. They usually have a coating of natural wax for maximum rigidity and easy pours. They tend to burn with a slight curl that creates a 'self-trimming' effect with minimal carbon build-up on the wick and a stable flame.

RAW WICKS

Made from unwaxed cotton, a raw wick is supplied in a spool. These wicks are great for taper candles and moulded candles.

WICK STICKERS

Wick stickers are double-sided, heat-resistant, sticky foam pads that you place on the bottom of pre-tabbed wicks to adhere your wick to the bottom of the candle container.

WICK POSITIONERS

To ensure that your candle wick is positioned straight throughout the candle, you need to secure it with a wick positioner. It is very important for the safety of the burning candle and performance that the wick is centred through the entire candle. We use a few different methods to secure wicks, from lollipop (popsicle) sticks with a central hole, to clothes pegs (pins) and metal positioners. These are available online or you can get creative with what you have to hand!

SUSTAINERS

In general, it is easier to use pre-tabbed wicks but if you need to make a custom wick then you can secure it with a metal tab, or wick sustainer. To use, thread a wick through the hole in the middle and crimp the wick into the sustainer using pliers. If using a wooden wick, simply slide it into the sustainer.

MULTI-WICK CANDLES

We recommend using multiple wicks in jars or containers that are larger than 9cm (3½in.) in diameter. Most wicks will struggle to create a melt pool larger than 7–9cm (3–3½in.), which means you need to use multiple wicks to melt all the way to the edges of your container.

Fragrance

Fragrance is one of the most exciting but complex parts of candle making. Whilst you truly have artistic licence when it comes to creating and blending a scent, you require a basic understanding of certain aspects of the craft to make it a success. When it comes to fragrance this is where both the art and science of candle making come into play.

Types of Fragrance

Fragrances are a mixture of chemicals (either natural or synthetic) designed to emit a smell. The way these chemical mixtures are deciphered by our brain is what translates the mixture into a fragrance we enjoy (or don't). Whether natural or synthetic, each fragrance will be made up of hundreds of molecules. When making candles, you can work with either fragrance oils or essential oils – let's look in more detail at the difference between these fragrance types and best-suited uses.

In our practice, we use a mixture of both essential oils and fragrance oils in order to create a well-rounded range. Some of our scents are essential oil only and some are made with fragrance oils. We don't want to tell you that one type of fragrance is better than another, however it's good to know the difference and decide what is important to you.

FRAGRANCE OILS

These oils are created synthetically rather than extracted from a natural source. Some fragrance oils contain a percentage of essential oils and various chemical components, which means that they can be formulated to replicate scents that are found in nature, such as pine or lemon. One of the benefits of fragrance oils is that they can emulate scents or concepts that cannot be derived by natural means, such as the scent of 'cappuccino' or the concept of 'fresh linen'.

Fragrance oils are basically created for candle making, which is what makes them easy to work with and, due to the fact that they are engineered, you are able to source a wide range of different scents to work with.

ESSENTIAL OILS

These oils are extracted (usually by steam or a cold-press process) directly from plants, using flowers, berries or herbs, and even needles, roots, peel and other parts of the plant. One of the benefits of essential oils is that they contain therapeutic and mood-boosting properties, for example lavender essential oil has been shown to have relaxing properties and citrus is well known to be invigorating and energizing. Essential oils tend to give off slightly less scent when burning than a fragrance oil, this is due to the fact that essential oils evaporate quickly. However, if making an all-natural candle is important to you then this is the best option.

FRAGRANCE BLENDS

It is possible to purchase pre-blended fragrances. Many of these fragrances are complex blends of several notes to give the fragrance depth and body. This is perfect if you want to create a candle really quickly but if you want to play around with mixing fragrance blends together, this is also a wonderful way to make a scent that is unique and robust.

Blending Your Own Fragrances

When blending and creating a fragrance, you truly have free rein. As a starting point, think about what memory, feeling or place you wish to evoke with the scent you are making.

BLENDING USING TOP, MIDDLE AND BASE NOTES

Different oils have different scent characteristics. To help blend scents effectively they can be categorized into Top Notes, Middle Notes and Base Notes. Top-note scents usually work fast and evaporate fast – they are what you smell first. Middle-note scents tend to be softer, warmer and full bodied. They are known for giving the heart to an oil blend along with a balancing effect. Base notes last a long time and evaporate more slowly. Base notes also have the effect of slowing down the evaporation of top- and mid-note oils. They are heavy, rich, solid and give your blend depth.

You don't have to stick to the top, middle, base-note method, but it is a good place to begin! It sometimes takes many attempts to perfect a scent blend so experiment and have fun.

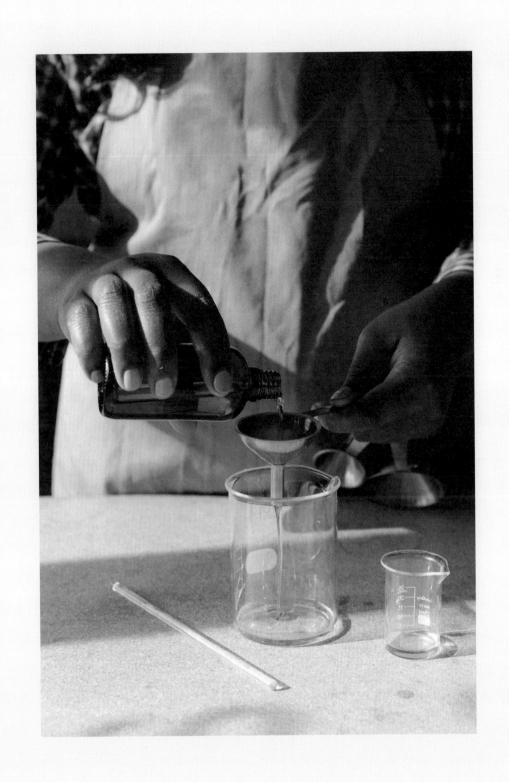

Examples of Fragrances and Their Note Categories:

TOP NOTES	Basil *(top-middle)*, Bergamot *(top-middle)*, Cinnamon, Clary Sage *(top-middle)*, Eucalyptus, Grapefruit, Lemon, Lemongrass *(top-middle)*, Lime, Mandarin, Neroli *(top-middle)*, Orange, Peppermint, Petitgrain, Tea Tree *(top-middle)*
MIDDLE NOTES	Black Pepper, Chamomile, Geranium, Juniper Berry, Lavender, Rosemary
BASE NOTES	Cedarwood, Cinnamon *(can be top, middle or base)*, Clove, Frankincense, Jasmine, Myrrh, Neroli *(can be top, middle or base)*, Patchouli, Rose, Sandalwood, Vanilla, Vetiver, Ylang Ylang *(base – middle)*

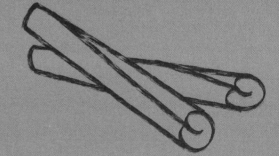

MIXING AN ESSENTIAL OIL BLEND

Here, we walk you through blending three oils – bergamot, lemon and mandarin – to make the Citrus Grove blend used in the wax melts project on page 60.

When measuring out oils, we like to use digital scales as it tends to be the most accurate method. Select the liquid measurement if your scale has this option, alternatively use weights in grams (or ounces). For the purposes of candle making, weight and liquid measures are equivalent, so 5ml (0.2fl oz) is equivalent to 5g (0.2oz).

Place your glass beaker on the digital scale and tare the weight. Using a pipette, extract your essential oils from their bottle and weigh out 3ml (0.1fl oz) of bergamot oil. Once you have done that, zero your scales again and, into the same beaker, add 2ml (0.07fl oz) of lemon oil. Zero the scales once more and add 5ml (0.2fl oz) of mandarin oil. Once all the oils have been measured out, stir thoroughly to ensure they are fully mixed together and combined.

Blending Using Scent Families

Another way to consider blending your fragrance is by combining scents that have roots in similar scent families. For example, blending a number of floral fragrances together, or blending a number of citrus fragrances together. This is a great method to use to create a harmonious blend.

SCENT FAMILY EXAMPLES

CITRUS – Bergamot, Grapefruit, Lemon, Lemongrass, Lime, Orange

FLORAL – Jasmine, Lavender, Rose

EARTHY – Moss, Orris Root, Vetiver

RESINOUS – Amber, Benzoin, Frankincense, Myrrh

WOODY – Cedarwood, Oak, Teakwood

HERBACEOUS – Basil, Marjoram, Rosemary, Sage

SPICY – Cardamom, Cinnamon, Ginger

Fragrance Load Calculation

Candle making is as much a science as it is an art. While you certainly have creative licence, it is important to keep things accurate when it comes to fragrance. So how much fragrance do you add to your candle?

Fragrance load is calculated in percentages. Each wax type has a maximum percentage of fragrance it can take. When purchasing wax, take note of this information to ensure that you don't exceed the maximum. Finding the best percentage for your candle is really a case of personal taste and trial and error.

The higher percentage you choose, the stronger the scent throw. We typically don't exceed 10 per cent fragrance load and have found that our sweet spot is somewhere between 6 and 8 per cent.

Try this simple formula:

(g/oz of wax) x (% of fragrance oil) = (ml/fl oz of fragrance oil needed)

For example, 700g (25oz) of wax x 8% = 56ml (2fl oz) of fragrance oil

When purchasing fragrance oils, look for phthalate-free fragrances and suppliers that are accredited as cruelty free. Also, check that the oils meet the standards set by the International Fragrance Association (IFRA).

With essential oils, although they are natural, it's important to remember that the oils are a highly concentrated version of the essence found in one plant, so take care in handling the individual oils to avoid contact or inhalation. If possible, wear protective gloves and ensure you are working in a well- ventilated room.

Dyes

Adding colour to your candle is a great way to introduce some personality to your projects! There are two types of dyes that you can use for your candle projects: chip or powder dye, and liquid dye. We love powder dyes as they tend to have minimal impact on burn performance and are easy to use. Dyes are another element that requires a little trial and error to get the colour exactly as you want. To dye your wax, a simple method to apply is to use the dye at a concentration of 1%. This means that 10g (0.3oz) powder candle dye will colour approximately 1kg (35oz) of wax.

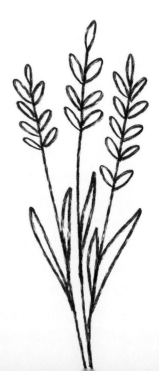

Equipment

We have put together a basic list of equipment you'll need to get started on your candle-making journey.

• JUG FOR MELTING WAX
Jugs created specifically for candle making are usually metal. You can also use a glass or plastic jug but a metal jug is easier to clean.

• WEIGHING SCALES
For making candles for personal use, you can use digital kitchen scales, however if you plan to sell your candles, we would advise investing in accurate trading scales.

• HEATPROOF BOWL OR JUG
  (CUP OR PITCHER)
Use this to melt your wax in the double-boiler method (see page 27); it's always best to avoid direct heat when melting wax to ensure it doesn't burn.

• SAUCEPAN
Use in combination with your bowl or jug to melt your wax on a stovetop.

• DOUBLE BOILER
You can purchase a dedicated double-boiler pan and keep this specifically for your candle-making projects.

• THERMOMETER
Use a thermometer, such as a sugar candy thermometer or a culinary digital thermometer, to measure the optimum temperature so you know when to add scent and pour your wax. Specific thermometers for candle making are available that attach to the inside of the metal jug.

• PIPETTE AND BEAKER
Pipettes are commonly found in laboratories but are great for measuring out small quantities of oils when blending fragrances. A glass beaker, also used in laboratories, makes a useful container for holding your measured fragrance oil. A beaker with marked increments will help you to measure out liquid quantities, too.

• WOODEN OR SILICON
  SPOON OR SPATULA
To stir your molten wax; keep specifically for candle making.

• CLOTHES PEG (PIN)
  OR CHOPSTICKS
To secure your wick in place.

• GLUE GUN
An electric tool used for melting and applying sticks of glue. We use a glue gun to secure wicks to our jars or containers as an alternative to wick stickers.

• SCISSORS, NAIL CLIPPER
  OR WICK TRIMMER
To trim your wick to size.

• CANDLE CONTAINERS
We are huge fans of humble amber glass jars; they come in a good range of sizes and when lit they provide a beautiful amber glow. They can be found online alongside purpose-made candle containers, however for candle

making at home, you can use any vessel that is heatproof and sturdy – glass or ceramics work well.

• PISTON FUNNEL
This is a stainless-steel funnel used for accurate pouring and filling. It is primarily used for baking but is also great for candle making when pouring into small containers like tealight holders, or for pouring in situations where you need to be extra careful to avoid spillage.

• SPURTLE
The spurtle is a wooden Scottish kitchen tool, to stir your molten wax; keep specifically for candle making.

• HEAT GUN
A heat gun blows out hot air through a nozzle, working in a similar way to a hairdryer. We use heat guns to fix any flaws on the surface of the candle by remelting the top layer, allowing it to reset smoothly.

• TALL BUCKET
  OR CONTAINER
When making taper candles it is best to set aside a metal bucket to use for dipping; the deeper the bucket the longer the candles you can make.

Terminology

CURING — The period of time between pouring the candle and the candle reaching a state where it can be lit to give optimum performance. The curing time will differ for each wax/fragrance oil mixture.

CRYSTALLIZATION OR FROSTING — When white crystal-like formations appear on the surface of the candle during curing. This is a common occurrence when working with natural waxes like soy wax, and is usually caused by fluctuations in temperature as the wax cools and returns to its natural state. You can combat this by candle making in an ambient room or try pre-heating your jars to keep them warm while pouring in your molten wax to avoid a drastic temperature change.

DOUBLE POUR — A candle-pouring technique in which a container candle is poured in two stages. Typically, the first pour will fill 70–90 per cent of the candle. After cooling, when the wax has contracted, the second pour fills the candle to the desired level. This method ensures that the candle surface sets smoothly.

FRAGRANCE LOAD — The ratio of fragrance oil to wax. A fragrance load of 10 per cent means that the weight of fragrance oil used in the candle will be 10 per cent of the weight of wax used. For example, if a candle has a fragrance load of 10 per cent, then a candle that uses 90g of wax will require 9g of fragrance oil to be added to the wax (or for 3oz of wax you will need 0.3oz of oil).

FROSTING — The 'frosting' often referred to in candle making is an example of 'polymorphism', where the solid mass of wax and fragrance oil changes into a different crystal form over time, causing a frost-like effect on the surface of the candle. See also crystallization.

FULL MELT POOL (FMP) — When the melt pool in a container candle covers the entire surface of the candle.

HOT THROW — The fragrance emitted from a fragranced container candle when the candle is burning.

COLD THROW — The fragrance emitted from a fragranced container candle when the candle has not been lit. How strong it smells when you just pick it up and smell it!

SINK HOLE — A gap or void that is formed inside or on the surface of a candle as the wax contracts during the cooling and curing process.

TUNNELLING — When only the wax around the wick melts down through the centre of the candle. This indicates that the candle may be under-wicked (wick size too small) or that the wick is incompatible with the wax/fragrance oil mixture.

SAFETY GUIDELINES

*Candle making is definitely fun but it's important to keep safety in mind.
Follow these guidelines to keep yourself and your housemates safe.*

- *When working with fragrance or essential oils, work
  in a well-ventilated room to allow air to circulate*
- *Keep long hair tied back and long sleeves rolled up*
- *When working with liquids we recommend using goggles
  to protect your eyes*
- *Ensure young children and pets are kept away from your
  making station*
- *Never leave melting wax unattended*

Projects

Spring

Scents to explore: Fresh, Green, Light

Basil, Bergamot, Blackberry,
Geranium, Grapefruit, Lemon,
Mandarin, Mint, Sage

Morning Dawn Tealights

If you're new to candle making, tealight candles are a great place to begin. They're easy, can be coloured or fragranced to match the season, and add a lovely, flickering ambience to any space or special occasion. In Spring, these are a beautiful way to add some atmosphere to your table and are lovely for breakfast, lunch or dinner.

Makes approximately 20 tealight candles

2   You will need

400g (14oz) soy wax flakes
Approx. 20 x aluminium tealight cups
10ml (0.3fl oz) Grapefruit essential oil
10ml (0.3fl oz) Lemongrass essential oil

Approx. 20 x wick stickers, or a glue gun
Approx. 20 x pre-tabbed tealight wicks

Metal jug or heatproof bowl
Scales
Saucepan
Digital thermometer
Wooden spoon or spatula
Glass beaker and pipette (optional)
Piston funnel (optional)

4

Method

STEP 1

Place the metal pouring jug on your scale and tare the weight. Weigh out your wax and melt using the double-boiler method (see page 27). Stir until all the wax is melted.

STEP 2

While the wax melts, prepare your tealight cups. Attach a wick sticker to the metal tab of each of your pre-tabbed wicks. Place a wick in the centre of each tealight cup.

STEP 3

Once your wax has melted, remove the jug from the heat and rest it on a heatproof surface. Check the temperature and let it cool to 65°C (149°F), then add your fragrance. Measure out the quantities of oils into a glass beaker, using a pipette if you have one, then add to your melted wax. Use a wooden spoon or spatula to stir the fragrance and wax for 2 minutes to ensure the fragrance is thoroughly incorporated.

STEP 4

When the wax has cooled to between 50–60°C (122–140°F), working carefully and slowly, pour the wax from the metal jug into the prepared tealight cups. If you have a piston funnel, pour your wax into the funnel and then dispense into the tealight cups. This is optional, but makes it much easier to pour the small quantities of wax needed to fill the tealight cups.

STEP 5

Allow the tealights to cure overnight before burning them. Once your candles have set and trim the wicks to around 5mm (¼in.) in length.

Citrus Grove
Wax Melts

A wax melt is like a candle without the wick, designed to
be used with an oil burner. They have become increasingly
popular in recent years. The fact these are flameless means it
is a great way to scent your space around children and pets.
You also can control the strength of the aroma by adding
or removing melts to your burner and you can keep them
simple or have fun experimenting with colour
or different shapes.

Makes approximately 16 wax melts

You will need

100g (3½oz) soy wax flakes
3ml (0.1fl oz) Bergamot essential oil
2ml (0.07fl oz) Lemon essential oil
5ml (0.2fl oz) Mandarin essential oil
1g (0.04oz) candle dye, colour of your choice

Multiple silicon candle mould
  (an ice-cube tray works too)

Metal jug or heatproof bowl
Saucepan
Digital thermometer
Glass beaker
Pipette (optional)
Wooden spoon or spatula
Oil burner

Method

STEP 1

Place the metal pouring jug on your scale and tare the weight. Weigh out your wax and melt using the double-boiler method (see page 27). Stir until all the wax is melted. Once the wax is completely melted, remove the jug or bowl from the heat and rest it on a heatproof surface. Check the temperature and let it cool to 65°C (149°F).

STEP 2

Now it's time to add your colour and scent. Stir in 1g (0.04oz) of dye – a little goes a long way, so add gradually and mix until you've got your desired colour. Measure out the quantities of oils into a glass beaker, using a pipette if you have one, then add to your melted wax. Use a wooden spoon or spatula to stir the fragrance and wax for 2 minutes to ensure the fragrance is thoroughly incorporated.

STEP 3

When the wax has cooled to between 50–60°C (122–140°F), pour the wax into the silicon mould. Once you stir, the wax can cool quite quickly – don't let it cool too much or it will become too firm to pour into the moulds.

STEP 4

Leave your wax melts to set for 2 hours, then remove them from the moulds. Once they are out of the moulds, you can use them immediately but for best results leave them to set fully for 24–48 hours. This ensures the best, fullest aroma when you use them.

STEP 5

To use your wax melts, pop one or two into the top of an oil burner, light a tealight underneath, and enjoy the fragrance that is released as the wax warms up and melts.

Botanical Bubble Candle

Moulded candles have become popular accessory in home interiors. With so many moulds available to buy you can create beautiful candle creations that are almost sculptural pieces, which will add an element of stylish decor in any room.

Makes 4 candles

1
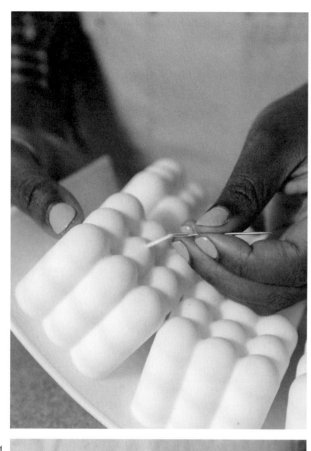

2
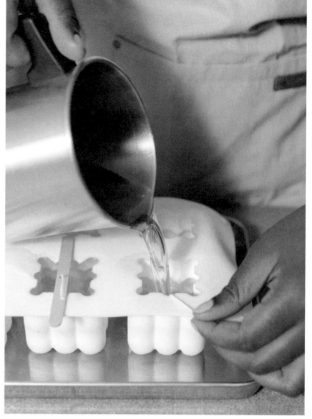

66

4
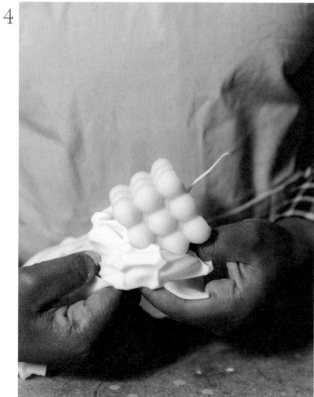

4.1

You will need

Spool of raw cotton wick
650g (1lb 7oz) soy wax flakes
  (pillar blend)
6.5g (0.2oz) candle dye, colour
  of your choice (optional)
60ml (2fl oz) floral fragrance
  oil blend

Silicon bubble candle mould
Yarn or tapestry needle
Lollipop (popsicle) stick or
  wick positioner

Metal jug
Weighing scales
Saucepan
Wooden spoon or spatula
Digital thermometer
Glass beaker and pipette
  (optional)
Rubber gloves (optional)

Method

STEP 1

First, get your wicks ready to thread through the mould. Measure out the desired wick length by turning your mould on its side and ensuring the length is long enough to go through the centre of the mould, leaving about 4cm (1½in.) on either side. Trim the wick to length. Make a hole in the centre of the mould if there isn't already one there, and thread the candle wick through using a needle. Hold the wick in place with a lollipop (popsicle) stick or wick positioner.

STEP 2

Place the metal pouring jug on your scale and tare the weight. Weigh out your wax and melt using the double-boiler method (see page 27). Stir until all the wax is melted. Once the wax is completely melted, remove the jug from the heat and rest it on a heatproof surface. Check the temperature and let it cool to 65°C (149°F), then add 6.5g (0.2oz) of dye – a little goes a long way, so add gradually and mix until you've got your desired colour.

STEP 3

Once you have mixed in your dye, measure out the quantity of oil into a glass beaker, using a pipette if you have one, then add to your melted wax. Use a wooden spoon or spatula to stir the fragrance and wax for 2 minutes to ensure the fragrance is thoroughly incorporated.

STEP 4

When the wax has cooled to between 45-50°C (113–122°F), pour it into the moulds very slowly and let it cool for 4-5 hours or overnight. Remove your candle from the mould very carefully, wearing gloves if possible, so that you don't affect the shape of the candle. Trim the wick to 5mm (¼in.), then your candle is ready to burn.

Rest and Recharge Aromatherapy Candle

Aromatherapy candles are made using pure essential oils (as opposed to fragrance oils). Each essential oil has its own therapeutic benefit. As the candle burns, the essential oils gently evaporate from the surface of the melting wax. Depending on the oils you've chosen, the essential oils may have uplifting, energizing, calming or invigorating properties.

Makes 2 container candles

You will need

530g (1lb 2oz) soy wax flakes
53ml (1.7fl oz) essential oil blend:
  • 25ml (0.8fl oz)
    Lavender essential oil
  • 22ml (0.7fl oz)
    Geranium essential oil
  • 6ml (0.2fl oz)
    Chamomile essential oil

2 x 30cl containers, glass
  or ceramic
4 x wick stickers, or a glue gun
4 x ECO 6 wicks, or similar
4 x wick positioners

Metal jug
Weighing scales
Saucepan
Wooden spoon or spatula
Digital thermometer
Glass beaker and pipette
  (optional)

Method

STEP 1

Place the metal pouring jug on your scale and tare the weight. Weigh out your wax and melt using the double-boiler method (see page 27). Stir until all the wax is melted.

STEP 2

While the wax melts, you can prepare your containers. Peel off one end of the wick sticker and stick it to the base of your wick, then place the wick in the centre of the container and firmly press so that it is securely stuck to the base.

STEP 3

Once the wax is completely melted, remove the jug or bowl from the heat and rest it on a heatproof surface. Check the temperature and let it cool to 60°C (140°F). Measure out the quantities of oils into a glass beaker, using a pipette if you have one, then add to your melted wax. Use a wooden spoon or spatula to stir the fragrance and wax for 2 minutes to ensure the fragrance is thoroughly incorporated.

STEP 4

Add your wick positioner to centre the wick and hold it in place. Repeat for all the containers. Check the temperature of the wax and when it has cooled to about 50–55°C (122–131°F), gently pour the wax into each container. Once the containers are topped up (see Tip, below), leave them to cool off for around 24 hours. After 24 hours the wax should have set nicely. Now it's time to remove the wick positioner and trim the wick to about 5mm (¼in.).

Tip:
When pouring the wax, leave some room at the top of the container and allow it to set for 30 minutes, then add the remaining wax. This way you'll make sure that the candles have smooth tops, as the second pour will fill any sink holes that might have formed.

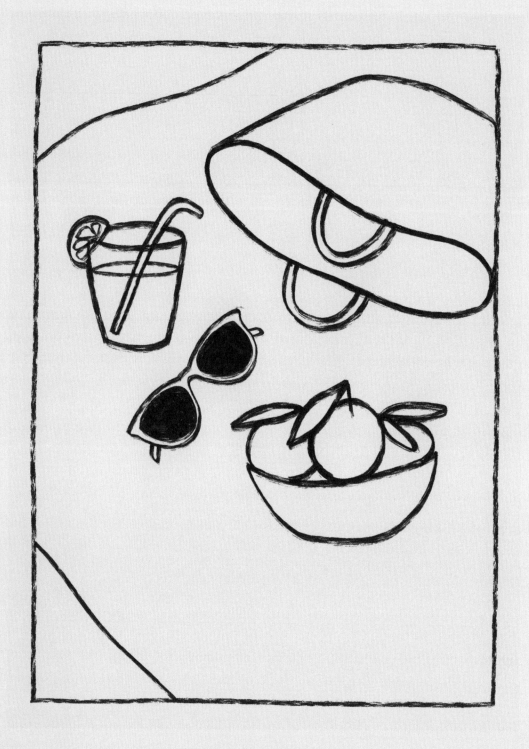

72

Summer

Scents to explore: Bright, Sweet, Fruity

Blossom, Citronella, Coconut, Gardenia, Grapefruit, Grass, Orange, Peach, Raspberry, Ylang Ylang

Gather Together
Taper Candle

Tapered candles is one of our favourite ways to dress
a dinner table. They are great fun to create and can be made
in a variety of colours to go with your table setting. Summer
is a time for gatherings with friends and family, sharing
food, stories and laughs by candlelight.

Makes 6 tapered candles

You will need

1kg (35oz) beeswax pellets
10g (0.4oz) candle dye, colour
* of your choice (optional)*

Spool of raw cotton wick
6 x metal nuts or weights,
* such as a stone*
Length of wooden dowel
* or stick*

Weighing scales
Large saucepan
Metal jug, small saucepan
* or heatproof bowl*
Digital thermometer
Glass beaker and pipette
* (optional)*
Tall metal or glass jar,
* or a steel bucket*
Tall jug of cold water
Scissors or a craft knife

Tip:
When you are making a number
of candles, the volume of wax in
your container will inevitably
go down – sometimes this
means rings form around the
top of your candle. To avoid
this, top up your wax container
regularly to keep it at the same
level, ensuring your candles
stay smooth.

Method

STEP 1
Fill a large saucepan with water and bring to the boil. Pour your measured wax into a melting jug and melt using the double-boiler method (see page 27). Once melted, keep the jug on a low heat to keep the wax heated throughout the process.

STEP 2
Add the dye to your molten wax – a little goes a long way, so add gradually and mix until you've got your desired colour – we have chosen a rose pink for our candles. Use a wooden spoon or spatula to stir the dye and wax for 2 minutes to ensure the dye is thoroughly incorporated.

STEP 3
Trim your wicks to double the desired length of your taper candles: the length you cut will be used to make two candles being dipped simultaneously. In this project we cut our wicks to about 50cm (20in.), and folded in half. Make sure to leave lots of extra space for you to safely hold the wick without coming into contact with any hot wax, and an extra 2cm (¾in.) that will remain to be lit once the candle is finished.

STEP 4
Attach a metal nut or a stone to the end of your wick to help keep the wick straight during the dipping process, tie one to both ends of the wick. You can hold your wicks by the folded part of the wick or hang your wicks from the central fold over a wooden dowel or stick. You can dip multiple candles at the same time if you hang a few lengths of wick onto a wooden dowel and dip into the wax simultaneously.

STEP 5
Dip the wicks into the molten wax. Hold the wicks submerged in the wax until air bubbles appear. When the air bubbles have stopped entirely, remove the wick from the wax, ensuring each length is covered in wax, and straighten them out by hand. Let the wax cool.

STEP 6
Once coated in wax, dip the wicks into the jug of cold water to set the wax. Dip again in the molten wax, then dip into the water jug to set. Keep alternating between the wax and water jug until the candle has reached the desired thickness; the tapered shape will develop naturally. When they've reached the desired thickness, leave your candles to dry for 12 hours.

STEP 7
When dry, cut the wick to separate the two candles and trim the wick on each down to the desired length. Use scissors or a craft knife to straighten off the base of the candle and remove the weight.

Sunny Citronella Outdoor Candle

Living in Scotland, any time the sun is out (which isn't often!) we definitely make the most of it by getting outdoors. To keep bugs and midges away from seating areas and food, a citronella candle is a great project to try! You can repurpose old food cans for this as they make the perfect vessel for an outdoor candle. Citronella's rich, crisp, lemony aroma also induces feelings of freshness, happiness and hope.

Makes 1 large tin candle

You will need

Stabilo 18 wick, or similar
460g (13oz) soy wax flakes
90g (3oz) beeswax pellets
45ml (1.5fl oz) Citronella
*   essential oil*

Repurposed metal tin or can
Glue gun or a wick sticker
Wick positioner

Metal jug
Weighing scales
Saucepan
Wooden spoon or spatula
Digital thermometer
Glass beaker and pipette
*   (optional)*
Heat gun (optional)

Method

STEP 1
Add the wick to the centre of the tin or container. We like to use a glue gun for this project but if you don't have one to hand you can use a wick sticker to secure your wick.

STEP 2
For this project we blend soy wax with beeswax. This raises the melting point of the wax to a high enough temperature to stay solid during warmer summer weather. Place the metal jug on your scale and tare the weight. Weigh out your wax and melt using the double-boiler method (see page 27). Stir until all the wax is melted.

STEP 3
Once the wax is completely melted, remove the jug or bowl from the heat and rest it on a heatproof surface. Check the temperature and let it cool to 65°C (149°F). Once it has cooled, add the citronella fragrance oil and use a wooden spoon or spatula to stir the fragrance and wax for 2 minutes to ensure the fragrance is thoroughly incorporated.

STEP 4
When the wax has cooled to between 55–60°C (131–140°F), carefully pour the wax mixture into the candle tin. Using a wick positioner, straighten and centre the wick in the tin and allow the candle to cool at room temperature overnight.

STEP 5
After the wax has completely cooled, remove the wick positioner and trim the wick to about 5mm (¼in.). If necessary, you can smooth the top of the candle using a heat gun (or hairdryer) to rectify any cracks or dips.

Summer Glow Pressed Flower Candle

This is a lovely hands-on activity and makes a great craft to try with older children. You can purchase pressed and dried flowers, or pick your own and dry thoroughly by hanging upside down in a dark room. To press the flowers, just place the dried flowers in a book and keep there until flattened. When lit, these candles give off a beautiful summery glow through the dried flower petals.

Makes 2 container candles

You will need

530g (14oz) soy wax flakes
53ml (1.7fl oz) of your favourite
   summery fragrance oil

Clear glass jar or container,
   approx. 30cl (10fl oz)
PVA (white) glue
Paintbrush
Selection of dried and pressed flowers
Spool of ECO 12 wick, or similar
2 x wick stickers, or a glue gun
2 x wick positioners

Metal jug or pouring bowl
Metal jug
Weighing scales
Saucepan
Wooden spoon or spatula
Digital thermometer
Glass beaker and pipette
   (optional)
Heat gun (optional)

Tip:
The sensitivity to temperature and humidity in vegetable wax frequently creates irregular crystals on the top (bumps) and sides (frosting). Use a heat gun (or hairdryer) to melt the top layer, this allows it to set again smoothly.

Method

STEP 1
Paint a light layer of PVA glue onto the inner surface of your candle jar and affix your pressed flowers, making sure they are flat against the surface. Paint another light layer of glue over the flower to secure it in place. Repeat until you have arranged the flowers in a pattern over the inside. Once you are happy with your candle vessels, secure your wick in the centre of each jar using a glue gun or wick sticker.

STEP 2
Place the metal pouring jug on your scale and tare the weight. Weigh out your wax and melt using the double-boiler method (see page 27). Stir until all the wax is melted. Once the wax is completely melted, remove the jug or bowl from the heat and rest it on a heatproof surface.

STEP 3
Check the temperature and let it cool to 60–65 °C (140–149 °F). Add your fragrance and use a wooden spoon or spatula to stir the fragrance and wax for 2 minutes to ensure the fragrance is thoroughly incorporated.

STEP 4
Check that the PVA glue has dried completely and once it has and your wax is at about 50 °C (122 °F), you can fill your vessels. Use a wick positioner to straighten and centre the wick in the jars and allow the candles to cool at room temperature overnight. Trim the wicks to 5mm (¼in.), smooth the surfaces if needed with a heat gun (see Tip, above left), light, and enjoy!

Wanderlust Travel Candle

While travelling, bringing along some home comforts can help you relax into your new surroundings and what better way to do this than to pack a travel candle. We love to take these along when staying in rented accommodation, to make it instantly feel like home. These candles are housed in a tin with a lid – perfect for popping into your travel bag and getting on the road!

Makes 2 candles

You will need

350g (13oz) soy wax flakes
10ml (0.3fl oz) Cedarwood
  essential oil
15ml (0.5fl oz) Orange
  essential oil
10ml (0.3fl oz) Geranium
  essential oil

2 x spool of ECO 6 wick,
  or similar
5x wick stickers, or a glue gun
5 x wick positioners
5 x 20cl (6.7fl oz) travel tins
  (see suppliers on page 142)

Metal jug
Weighing scales
Saucepan
Wooden spoon or spatula
Digital thermometer
Glass beaker and pipette
  (optional)

Method

STEP 1
Place the metal pouring jug on your scale and tare the weight. Weigh out your wax and melt using the double-boiler method (see page 27). Stir until all the wax is melted.

STEP 2
While the wax melts, prepare your containers. Peel off one end of the wick sticker and stick it to the base of your wick, then place the wick in the centre of the tin and firmly press to securely stick it to the base. Then, use your wick positioner to hold the wick in place. Repeat for each of the containers.

STEP 3
Return to your melting pot and stir to ensure that the wax is thoroughly melted. Use the thermometer to measure the temperature, it should be about 60°C (140°F). Once the wax is completely melted, remove the jug or bowl from the heat and rest it on a heatproof surface.

STEP 4
Measure out the quantities of oils into a glass beaker, using a pipette if you have one, then add to your melted wax. Use a wooden spoon or spatula to stir the fragrance and wax for 2 minutes to ensure the fragrance is thoroughly incorporated.

STEP 5
Check that your wax temperature is around 50–55°C (122–131°F), then gently pour the wax into each tin. Leave to set for 24 hours. Once set, remove the wick positioner and trim the wick to around 5mm (¼in.). Place the lid on the tin and you're all set!

Coastal Seashell Candle

These decorative candles are a beautiful way to dress up
a mantlepiece or table. You can buy natural seashells online
or, if you're lucky enough to live near the sea, collect some on
a beachcombing expedition, give them a wash, and use them
for this project! This project makes 5 large shell candles, but
you can multiply up if you have more shells or divide the
mixture if your shells are smaller.

Makes 5 seashell candles

You will need

200g (7oz) soy wax flakes
20ml (0.7fl oz) Sea Salt and Sage fragrance oil

Wicks – size will depend on the diameter of your
*   shell; check the manufacturer's guide to choose*
*   an appropriate wick size: we used ECO 8 wicks*
*   for our 13cm (5in.) shell and ECO 6 wicks for*
*   the 6cm (2½in.) shells*
5 x seashells in assorted sizes, approx. 2 x 13cm
*   (5in.) and 3 x 6cm (2½in.) in diameter*
*   (flat, scallop shapes work best)*
5 x wick stickers, or a glue gun

Metal jug
Weighing scales
Saucepan
Wooden spoon or spatula
Digital thermometer
Glass beaker and pipette (optional)

2

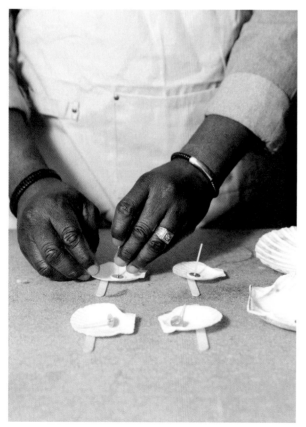

1

*Use lollipop (popsicle)
sticks beneath the shells to
keep them level and stop
them from tipping over
as you pour the wax.*

Method

STEP 1
Secure the wicks to the centre of the deepest part of each shell using a wick sticker or glue gun. Make sure the wicks are standing up straight and not bent over.

STEP 2
Place the metal pouring jug on your scale and tare the weight. Weigh out your wax and melt using the double-boiler method (see page 27). Stir until all the wax is melted. Once melted, use your thermometer to measure the wax's temperature, it should be about 60°C (140°F).

STEP 3
Measure out the quantities of oils into a glass beaker, using a pipette if you have one, then add to your melted wax. Use a wooden spoon or spatula to stir the fragrance and wax for 2 minutes to ensure the fragrance is thoroughly incorporated.

STEP 4
Check that the wax temperature is around 50–55°C (122–131°F), then gently pour the wax into each shell, taking care not to overfill and spill the wax over the edges. Leave the candles to set for 6 hours. Once set you are free to light up your candles and enjoy!

Autumn

Scents to explore: Earthy, Woody, Green, Gourmand

Apple, Black Pepper,
Cardamom, Cedarwood,
Coffee, Cypress, Eucalyptus,
Juniper, Nutmeg, Thyme,
Vetiver

Evening Glow Amber Container Candle

These candles are our bread and butter – they started our journey. This project takes us back to those early days of candle making on our kitchen counter, testing and blending. There is something so beautiful about that warm amber glow on a chilly autumn evening. The spicy and earthy scent is similar to our Road to Port Harcourt Candle, inspired by Emmanuel's home town in Nigeria.

Makes 4 container candles

You will need

850g (1lb 14oz) C3 soy wax flakes
45ml (1.5fl oz) Bergamot
  essential oil
5ml (0.2fl oz) Vetiver
  essential oil
5ml (0.2fl oz) Black Pepper
  essential oil

4 x 180ml amber glass jars
4 x ECO 8 wicks, or similar
4 x wick stickers, or a glue gun
4 x wick positioners

Metal jug
Weighing scales
Saucepan
Wooden spoon or spatula
Digital thermometer
Glass beaker and pipette
  (optional)

2

Tip:
When pouring, leave some room at the top of the container and leave it to set for 30 minutes, then add the remaining wax. This way you'll make sure that the candles have smooth tops as the second pour will fill any sink holes that might have formed.

Method

STEP 1

Place the metal pouring jug on your scale and tare the weight. Weigh out your wax and melt using the double-boiler method (see page 27). Stir until all the wax is melted.

STEP 2

While the wax melts, you can prepare your containers. Peel off one end of the wick sticker and stick it to the base of your wick, then place the wick in the centre of the container and firmly press to securely stick it to the base. Then, use your wick positioner to hold the wick in place. Repeat for the remaining containers.

STEP 3

Measure out the quantities of oils into a glass beaker, using a pipette if you have one, then add to your melted wax. Use a wooden spoon or spatula to stir the fragrance and wax for 2 minutes to ensure the fragrance is thoroughly incorporated.

STEP 4

Check the temperature of the wax and when it has cooled to about 50–55°C (122–131°F), gently pour the wax into each container. Once the containers are topped up (see Tip, opposite), leave them to cure for around 24 hours. When the wax has set, remove the wick positioner and trim the wick to 5mm (¼in.).

2.1

Beeswax
Wrap Candles

This project is infinitely adaptable; you can make the candles to any length, simply rolled or tapered. Instead of using the dipping method, these candles use beeswax sheets, which don't require heat or melting, and produce minimal mess, making it a great, safe project to do with children on a rainy day. Beeswax candles have a warming, natural honey-like scent that is comforting and mellow, perfect for autumn.

Makes 2 candles

Short stumpy candle

You will need

*Beeswax sheets (approx.
20 x 40cm/8 x 16in.)*
*Spool of raw braided wicks
size 2/0, or similar*

Ruler
Craft knife or scissors

Method

STEP 1

Using your ruler as a guide and a craft knife, cut the beeswax sheet in half. Each section should measure 18 x 20cm (3 x 8in.). Place the two halves together and cut in half again. Each section should now measure 10 x 15cm (4 x 6in.). Line up your wick along one of the edges of the wax sheet, about 1cm (½in.) in from the edge of the sheet. Trim the wick, leaving about 2.5cm (1in.) of wick at either end.

STEP 2

Using your fingers, press the wick into one of the edges and begin to roll the wax sheet around the wick and away from you. Try not to apply too much pressure but keep the roll tight around the wick to ensure there are no gaps (which means that your candle will burn cleanly).

———————→

STEP 3

Once you have finished rolling the candle, press the edge into the candle. As beeswax is naturally sticky it should hold in place. Trim the bottom wick so that it is level with the base of the candle and trim the top wick to about a 5mm (¼in.). You are ready to light and enjoy your candle!

Tip:
You can cut multiple sheets and use the same overlapping and rolling method as many times as you want. The more sheets you add, the thicker your candle.

Rolled taper candle

STEP 1

This method is much the same as above, however the beeswax sheets are cut in a different way to achieve the tapered effect. Cut the beeswax sheet into two 20-cm (8-in.) squares.

STEP 2

Take one of the squares and position your ruler about 2.5cm (1in.) above the bottom edge, and cut a straight line diagonally to the top corner. Discard the smaller piece and use the larger shape for your candle.

STEP 3

Press a length of wick along the bottom edge, following the instructions in Steps 2 and 3 on the previous page and above, to finish the candle.

Tip:
Try to work in a warm room for this project as it helps the wax to stay pliable.

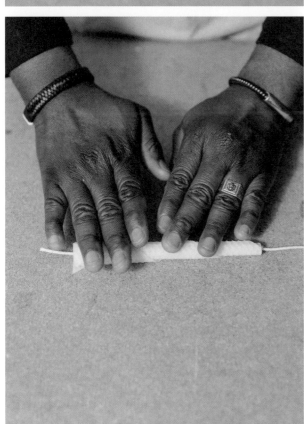

Fireside Wooden Wick Candle

Autumn is the perfect time of year to use wooden, rather than braided, wicks. You can imagine you're beside a tiny fire; the crackle of the wood wick is similar to the sound from wood logs burning in a fireplace. Pair this crackling sound with your favourite autumnal scents and prepare for a cosy evening.

Makes 2 container candles

You will need

700g (1lb 8oz) soy wax flakes
70ml (2.4fl oz) Spiced Apple
   fragrance oil

2 x 30cl (10fl oz) glass
   containers
4 x wooden wicks (check the
   manufacturer's guide to choose
   an appropriate wick size for
   your diameter of candle)
2 x metal wooden wick
   sustainers
2 x wick stickers, or a glue gun

Metal jug
Weighing scales
Saucepan
Wooden spoon or spatula
Digital thermometer
Glass beaker and pipette
   (optional)

1

Method

STEP 1
Place the metal pouring jug on your scale and tare the weight. Weigh out your wax and melt using the double-boiler method (see page 27). Stir until all the wax is melted.

STEP 2
Take two matching wicks and place them together in a metal sustainer. Once the wax has melted, dip the wooden wick into the molten wax, making sure that both sides are fully covered. Put these wicks to one side to allow the wax to cool and set. This should only take a few minutes.

STEP 3
Once the wax is completely melted, remove the jug or bowl from the heat and rest it on a heatproof surface. Check the temperature and let it cool to 65°C (149°F). Add the fragrance oil and use a wooden spoon or spatula to stir the fragrance and wax for 2 minutes to ensure the fragrance is thoroughly incorporated.

STEP 4
Trim the wick to 5mm (¼in.) and leave to set overnight.

2

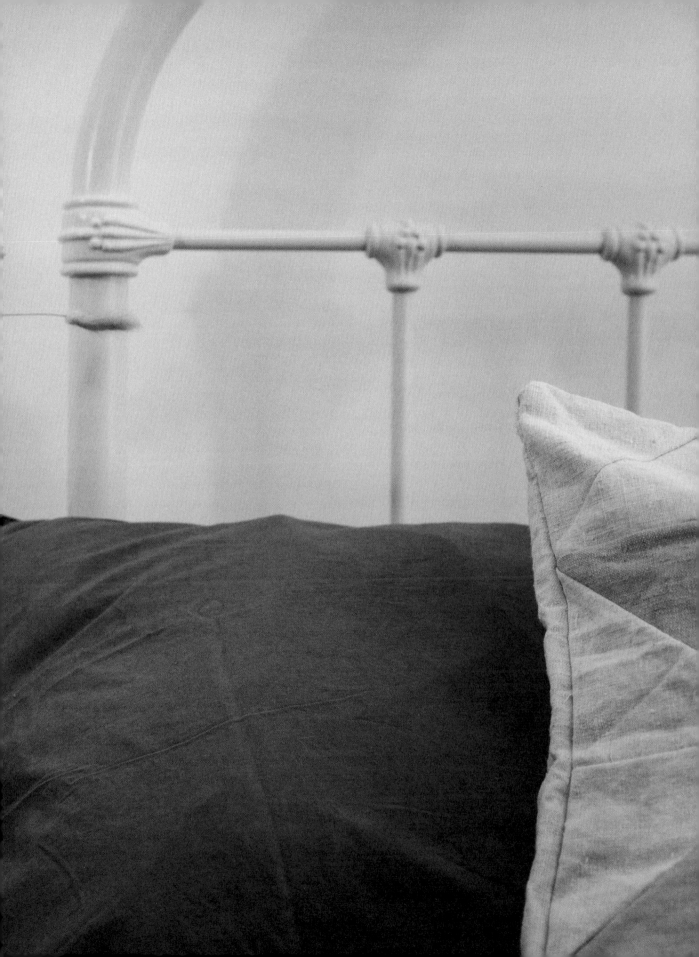

Twisted
Candle

Autumn mantlepieces, evening dinners, coffee table decor – these twisted candles are a beautiful talking point with an elegant design. You can personalize them by colouring them to match your decor or theme.

Makes approximately 6 twisted candles

You will need

1kg (2lb 4oz) beeswax pellets
10g (0.4oz) candle dye, colour
  of your choice (optional)

6 x unbleached raw candle wicks
6 x metal nuts or weights, such
  as a stone
Length of wooden dowel or stick

Metal jug
Weighing scales
Saucepan
Wooden spoon or spatula
Digital thermometer
Tall metal or glass jar,
  or steel bucket
Tall jug of cold water
Craft knife

Method

STEP 1
Fill a large saucepan with water and bring to the boil. Pour your measured wax into a melting jug and melt using the double-boiler method (see page 27). Once melted, keep the jug on a low heat to keep the wax heated throughout the process.

STEP 2
Add the dye to your molten wax – a little goes a long way, so add gradually and mix until you've got your desired colour. Use a wooden spoon or spatula to stir the dye and wax for 2 minutes to ensure the dye is thoroughly incorporated.

STEP 3
Trim your wicks to the desired length of your taper candles. In this project we cut our wicks to about 50cm (20in.), and folded in half. Make sure to leave lots of extra space for you to safely hold the wick without coming into contact with any hot wax, and an extra 2cm (¾in.) that will remain to be lit once the candle is finished.

STEP 4
Attach a metal nut or a stone to the end of your wick (see page 78) to help keep the wick straight during the dipping process, tie one to both ends of the wick. You can hold your wicks by the folded part of the wick or hang your wicks from the central fold over a wooden dowel or stick. You can dip multiple candles at the same time if you hang a few lengths of wick onto a wooden dowel and dip into the wax simultaneously.

STEP 5
Dip the wicks into the molten wax. Hold the wicks submerged in the wax until air bubbles appear. When the air bubbles have stopped entirely, remove the wick from the wax, ensuring each length is covered in wax, and straighten them out by hand. Let the wax cool. Continue to dip the wicks into the wax until your candles have reached the desired thickness.

STEP 6
While the candles are still warm, twist a pair together to make a spiral. It is easier to do this while the candles are submerged in warm water to keep them pliable and to prevent them from cracking.

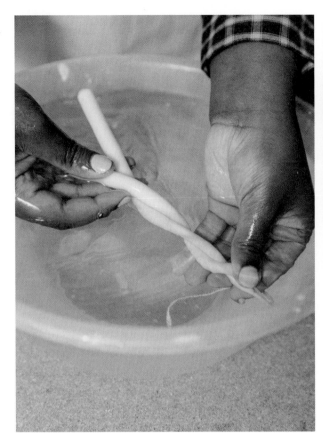

STEP 7

Dip them in the molten wax once more to seal them together and then hang them to dry for a few more hours. When dry, cut the wick to separate the two candles and trim the wick on each down to the desired length. Use a craft knife to straighten off the base of the candle and remove the weight.

> *Tip:*
> *Dip the candles into another*
> *bucket of cool water to get them*
> *to cool faster between each layer.*

Winter

Scents to explore: Spicy, Woody, Fresh

Anise, Cinnamon,
Frankincense, Myrrh,
Peppermint, Pine, Sandalwood,
Spruce, Vanilla

Winter Spice Three-wick Candle

The three-wick candle is a perfect way to scent large or open-plan spaces, and fits the bill if you like a good strong scent throw. For this candle we have created a festive blend celebrating the joy of the winter months – the scent of fresh bakes, winter markets and cosy evenings in.

Makes 1 container candle

125

WINTERWINTER

You will need

450g (1lb) soy wax flakes
20ml (0.7fl oz) Cinnamon
*   essential oil*
5ml (0.2fl oz) Clove Bud
*   essential oil*
5ml (0.2fl oz) Ginger
*   essential oil*
20ml (0.7fl oz) Orange
*   essential oil*

50 cl (17fl oz) glass candle dish,
*   our dish measured approx.*
*   13cm (5in.) diameter*
Glue gun or wick stickers
Glue dots
Lollipop (popsicle) stick wick
*   positioners*
3 x Eco 10 wicks

Metal jug
Weighing scales
Saucepan
Wooden spoon or spatula
Sheet of paper, pencil, ruler
Digital thermometer
Glass beaker and pipette
*   (optional)*

Method

STEP 1
Place the metal pouring jug on your scale and tare the weight. Weigh out your wax and melt using the double-boiler method (see page 27). Stir until all the wax is melted.

STEP 2
Draw a template to work out the best place to place the wicks. The easiest way to do this is to take a piece of paper and draw around the bottom of your container. Mark three dots in a triangle formation in the centre of the circle, using a ruler to ensure the dots are about 4cm (1½in.) away from each other.

STEP 3
Place your container over the template and stick your wick stickers or dots of glue to match the marked triangle. Attach the wicks to the stickers. Create a custom wick positioner by gluing three lollipop (popsicle) sticks into a triangle formation.

STEP 4
Once the wax is completely melted, remove the jug or bowl from the heat and rest it on a heatproof surface. Check the temperature and let it cool to 65°C (149°F). Measure out the quantities of oils into a glass beaker, using a pipette if you have one, then add to your melted wax. Use a wooden spoon or spatula to stir the fragrance and wax for 2 minutes to ensure the fragrance is thoroughly incorporated.

STEP 5
Let the wax cool to around 50–55°C (120–131°F) and carefully pour your wax into the container. Leave some room at the top so that you can do a second pour. After 30 minutes, pour the rest of your wax into the container to top up any sink holes or cracks that might have formed.

STEP 6
Use your wick positioning triangle to hold the wicks in place and leave to set for 24 hours. Trim the wicks to 5mm (¼in.), light and enjoy!

127

Festive Centrepiece Candle

Bring some wow factor to tables and gatherings with this extra-large centrepiece candle that exudes warmth and light in the winter months. For this project, we used a large ceramic bowl which was originally a serving dish to create this striking centrepiece.

Makes one extra-large container candle

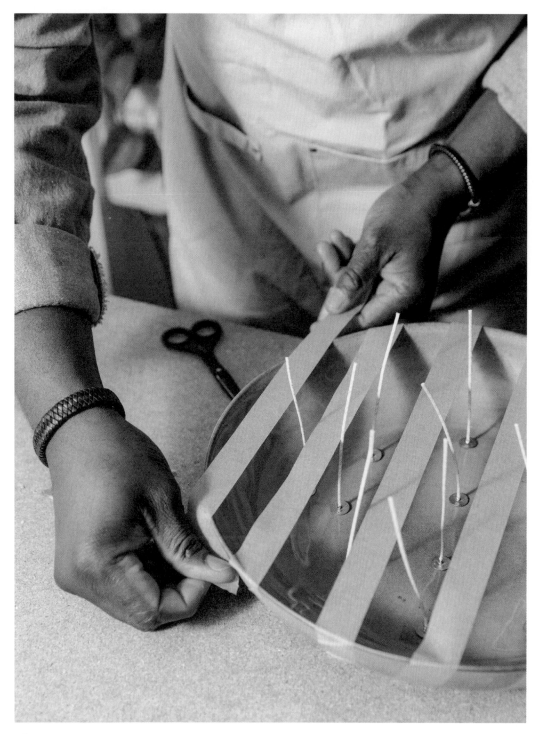

2

You will need

800g (1¾lb) soy wax flakes
Glazed ceramic dish, 34cm
  (13½in.) diameter
64ml (9fl oz) of any woody
  fragrance/essential oil blend

Marker pen
Wick stickers, or a glue gun
12 x Eco 12 wicks, or similar
Masking tape
Lollipop(popsicle) stick
  wick positioners

Metal jug
Weighing scales
Saucepan
Wooden spoon or spatula
Digital thermometer
Piston funnel (optional)

Tip:
*If you're using a ceramic
container, make sure it is
glazed and non-porous.
Unglazed materials, such as
clay flower pots, can sometimes
encourage the flame to grow to
the rim of your container, and
you could end up with a much
bigger flame than intended.*

*For a festive touch, place your
candle in the centre of a table
wreath or wrap foliage and
festive elements on the table
around the container.*

Method

STEP 1

Place the metal pouring jug on your scale and tare the weight. Weigh out your wax and melt using the double-boiler method (see page 27). Stir until all the wax is melted.

STEP 2

It is important to plan where you're going to place your wicks. If your container is transparent, follow the instructions for making a template on page 126. If your container is ceramic, take a marker pen and place dots about 4cm (1½in.) apart on the inside of the dish, ensuring they aren't too close to each other or too near the edge. Once you have planned the positions for your wicks, apply your wick stickers or dots of glue from a glue gun over the marked positions, and then affix your wicks to the base.

STEP 3

Create a wick positioner by attaching strips of masking tape across the dish. Then thread the lollipop (popsicle) wick positioners onto the wicks, to keep them upright, using the tape to hold them in position (see image on page 127).

STEP 4

Once the wax is completely melted, remove the jug or bowl from the heat and rest it on a heatproof surface. Check the temperature and let it cool to 65°C (149°F). Next, add in your essential or fragrance oils. Use a wooden spoon or spatula to stir the fragrance and wax for 2 minutes to ensure the fragrance is thoroughly incorporated.

STEP 5

When the wax has cooled to between 50–60°C (130–140°F), carefully pour it into the container; a piston funnel will help you pour through the small gaps. Leave some room at the top so that you can do a second pour. After 30 minutes, pour the rest of your wax into the container to top up any sink holes or cracks that might have formed. Leave to set for 24 hours then remove the masking tape and wick positioners, trim your wicks to 5mm (¼in.), light and enjoy!

Into the Woods
Pillar Candle

Pillar candles have a solid presence that suits both indoor and outdoor use. They are often found combined with storm lanterns, which protect the flame from draughts and keeps candles safe if used at floor level – they look particularly effective in fireplaces or on patios. We have added a fresh, green dye to our candle, alongside a pine fragrance, to bring the woods to you.

Makes 1 pillar candle

You will need

*630g (1lb 6oz) Pillar Blend
   soy wax*
44ml (1.5fl oz) Pine fragrance oil
*6.3g (0.2oz) candle dye, colour
   of your choice*

*Pillar mould approx. 6.5cm
   (2½in.) diameter, 22cm
   (9in.) high*
Raw LX 18 wick, or similar
Putty or sticky tack
*Wick positioner or cocktail
   stick (toothpick)*

Metal jug
Weighing scales
Saucepan
Wooden spoon or spatula
Digital thermometer
Metal skewer

Method

STEP 1
Place the metal pouring jug on your scale and tare the weight. Weigh out your wax and melt using the double-boiler method (see page 27). Stir until all the wax is melted.

STEP 2
While the wax is melting prepare your container and set the wick in place. The position might vary depending on the kind of mould you have, but typically you thread your wick through the wick hole in the mould and use a little putty or sticky tack to plug any gaps around the hole. Support the other end of the wick using a wick positioner, ensuring the wick is centred in the mould.

STEP 3
Once the wax is completely melted, remove the jug or bowl from the heat and rest it on a heatproof surface. Check the temperature and let it cool to 65°C (149°F). dissolves evenly and to avoid air bubbles.

1

2

STEP 4
Check the temperature again and when the wax is about 60°C (140°F), add in your fragrance. Use a wooden spoon or spatula to stir the fragrance and wax for 2 minutes to ensure the fragrance is thoroughly incorporated.

STEP 5
Now pour your wax slowly into the mould. It is really important to pour slowly to reduce the risk of air bubbles or pockets forming. Fill the container all the way to the top, or to about 2.5cm (1in.) below the top, leaving some room at the top so that you can do a second pour. After 30 minutes, pour the rest of your wax into the container to top up any sink holes or cracks that might have formed.

STEP 6
Leave to set on a flat surface for about 20–30 minutes. Once the cooled wax has formed a surface, use a skewer to poke some relief holes positioned around the wick. The holes should go almost all the way to the bottom of the candle, stopping approximately 2.5cm (1in.) from the base. Relief holes prevent air pockets and issues with the wick. Leave the candle to cool and set for between 12 and 24 hours when it should be cool enough to release from the mould. Trim your wick to 5mm (¼in.), then light and enjoy your candle.

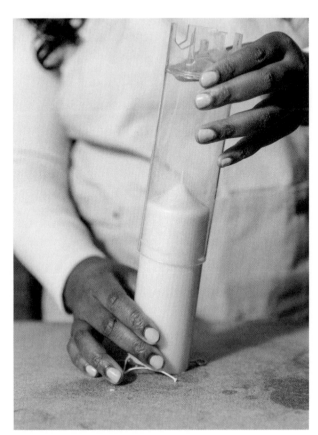

3

4

Work of Art Painted Candle

Hand-painted candles make a beautiful, decorative project that allows you to really get creative and craft something that fits in perfectly with your decor, the seasons or an occasion you might be celebrating – although these might just be too pretty to burn! For safe burning, use a water-based, non-toxic acrylic paint.

Makes 6 tapered candles

You will need

1kg (2lb 4oz) beeswax pellets
10g (0.4oz) candle dye, colour
  of your choice (optional)

6 x unbleached raw candle wicks
6 x metal nuts or weights, such
  as a stone
Length of wooden dowel or stick
Rubbing alcohol and cloth
Paintbrushes
Acrylic paints (water-based,
  non-toxic)

Weighing scales
Large saucepan
Metal jug, small saucepan
  or heatproof bowl
Digital thermometer
Tall metal or glass jar,
  or a steel bucket
Craft knife

Tip:
Think about using colours
and designs to match the
season; we've painted a simple,
abstract design featuring greens
and whites to represent the
natural colours of winter.

Method

STEP 1

Follow the instructions in the Gather Together Taper Candle project on page 76 to create your own dipped taper candles, or use any taper candles you have to hand. Prepare the surface of your candle by cleaning it with rubbing alcohol and a cloth. This helps to make the surface absorbent.

STEP 2

Paint your design straight onto the candle using a paintbrush or a sponge and acrylic paint. You can create your designs freehand or with paper stencils. You may need to apply a second coat of paint, or more, depending on the colour of paint and colour of your candle.

STEP 3

Leave your candle to dry for a few hours. Once the paint is dry, your candles are ready to display and use!

Recommended Suppliers

With the increasing popularity of candle making there are certainly many suppliers out there for you to explore. Part of the fun is discovering your favourite fragrances and waxes to work with, so take a look at what's available and do some research. Below we have listed a few tried-and-tested favourites of our own, to get you started on your candle-making journey.

C WYNNE JONES – jars
cwynnejones.com

CANDLE SHACK – essential oil blends, fragrance oils, candle jars
candle-shack.co.uk

CRAFTOVATOR – fragrance oils
craftovator.co.uk

FRESHSKIN – essential oils
freshskin.co.uk

LIVEMOOR – wax
livemoor.co.uk

NAISSANCE – essential oils
naissance.com

SUPPLIES FOR CANDLES – fragrance oils & wax
suppliesforcandles.co.uk

Acknowledgments

This book is truly a dream come true. It wouldn't have been possible without the amazing support from our friends, family and team.

To the team at Quadrille, wow – thank you for believing in us and putting us forward to create this book, we are so honoured! It's been a journey but you've been a great support through it all! Thank you Olivia, for bringing our book to life through your amazing design, thanks to Harriet, Claire and Ore for the support, guidance and styling on our shoot days, and thanks to India and Magnus for the beautiful photography. Thank you to the Future Kept for your prop loan and Fauna Folk for the beautiful flowers.

To our team – thank you for always holding the fort down. We appreciate everything you do and your love and dedication to OLG.

To our customers – thank you! We are truly lucky to have customers who buy from us again and again and support everything we do. You have kept us going through the most trying of times and for that we are grateful.

$\longrightarrow$

From Emmanuel

The thought of having a book in my name is mind boggling and, honestly, writing this book was harder than I imagined but this turned out to be a beautiful project and soul-satisfying journey.

To my mum Taribi, thank you for showing me first hand perseverance and what it means to put in work to get results. To my sisters Sarah, Hannah and Stella, thank you for always cheering me all the way and being an inspiration for my living.

To our young queens Eliana and Elyse, for giving me a reason to strive to do more, I hope I will always make you girls proud.

I would like to thank my wife, co-author and business partner, Ebi, for dreaming and living out this reality with me, thank you for challenging the normal and making me go above and beyond.

To my Creator 'Yahweh', thank you.

Finally, a favourite proverb that has guided my life: "I have learnt that a grateful heart and a giving spirit, always receives perfect gifts."

From Ebi

What a journey it's been! I have dreamt of writing a book since I was a young girl. I was always inspired by my father, whose work ethic, passion and legacy motivate me every day. Miss you dad, thank you for everything you were in your time on earth.

To my mum, thank you for your unwavering support and for always celebrating me, thank you for always being ready to help anyway you can and for your prayers.

To my siblings, Eje, Efe and Effua – for the fun we have together and for always cheering me on.

Thank you to our daughters, Eliana and Elyse, you girls truly bring so much joy and laughter to our home and are the reason we do what we do. I am so proud to be your mum.

Thank you to my husband and partner in life, Emmanuel – thank you for always believing in me and for building this beautiful life with me.

And, finally, thanks and praise to God, from whom all blessings flow.

About Our Lovely Goods

Our Lovely Goods is an e-commerce lifestyle brand inspired by home, family and heritage. Founded by Ebi and Emmanuel in 2019, their collection includes hand-poured candles, skincare and homewares made in Nigeria, combining traditional craft with new designs. The brand is centred around helping you to celebrate the feeling of home.

ourlovelygoods.com
@ourlovelygoods

Managing Director Sarah Lavelle
Senior Commissioning Editor Harriet Butt
Assistant Editor Oreolu Grillo
Head of Design Claire Rochford
Designer Olivia Bush
Illustrator Natalia Burgess
Prop loan The Future Kept (thefuturekept.com)
Photographer India Hobson
Photographer's Assistant Magnus Edmondson
Head of Production Stephen Lang
Production Controller Sabeena Atchia

Published in 2022 by Quadrille,
an imprint of Hardie Grant Publishing

Quadrille
52–54 Southwark Street
London SE1 1UN
quadrille.com

Cataloguing in Publication Data: a catalogue record for this book is available from the British Library.

Text © Ebi and Emmanuel Sinteh 2022
Photography © India Hobson 2022
Illustrations © Natalia Burgess 2022
Design © Quadrille 2022

ISBN 978 1 78713893 3
Printed in China using soy inks

FSC
www.fsc.org

MIX
Paper from
responsible sources
FSC™ C020056